Contents

Words appearing in bold, **like this**, are explained in the Glossary.

The light of our lives

Sunlight sparkling off the sea. Stars twinkling in the night sky. House lights making our homes cosy and allowing us to carry on with all our activities even when it is dark outside. Floodlights illuminating the evening game of football, baseball, hockey or basketball, head- and tail-lights making it possible to drive around after dark – light is vital for so many of our activities.

Light for living

What sort of things do you enjoy doing? Whatever your interests, whether they include sport, reading, computer games, watching TV or almost anything else you can think of, light will be important to you. But light is vital to all life on Earth, not just people. Light from the Sun is the ultimate source of **energy** for almost all living things. Life as we know it would be impossible without light! Not only that, but light also enables us (and many other living things) to see and make sense of the world around us.

Great light
The Sun radiates huge amounts of energy to the Earth every day.

Natural light, artificial light

The main natural source of light here on Earth is the Sun. The Sun is a star, our own 'home star', if you like. It is immensely hot – white hot – and the light that comes from it is known as **white light**. Even though this white light has travelled 150 million kilometres (93 million miles) by the time it reaches us, it still has the power to blind us if we look directly into the Sun itself. Light travels at the amazing speed of 300,000 kilometres (186,000 miles) per second. If the Sun went out now, we would not notice the difference for around eight minutes – the time it takes light to travel from the surface of the Sun to the Earth – but then it would be very dark, and cold, and life on Earth would soon cease to exist.

Seeing Things

Light

Ann Fullick

Heinemann
LIBRARY

www.heinemann.co.uk/library
Visit our website to find out more information about **Heinemann Library** books.

To order:

 Phone 44 (0) 1865 888066

 Send a fax to 44 (0) 1865 314091

 Visit the Heinemann Bookshop at www.heinemann.co.uk/library to browse our catalogue and order online.

First published in Great Britain by Heinemann Library, Halley Court, Jordan Hill, Oxford OX2 8EJ, part of Harcourt Education Ltd. Heinemann is a registered trademark of Harcourt Education Ltd.

© Harcourt Education Ltd 2004
First published in paperback in 2006.

Editorial: Sarah Eason and Kathy Peltan
Design: Jo Hinton-Malivoire/Ascenders
Picture Research: Ruth Blair and Debra Weatherley
Production: Edward Moore

Originated by Ambassador Litho Ltd
Printed and bound in China by South China Printing Co. Ltd.

The paper used to print this book comes from sustainable sources.

ISBN 0 431 16743 5 (hardback)
08 07 06 05 04
10 9 8 7 6 5 4 3 2 1

ISBN 0 431 16750 8 (paperback)
09 08 07 06
10 9 8 7 6 5 4 3 2 1

British Library Cataloguing in Publication
Fullick, Ann
Seeing Things: Light. – (Everyday science)
535
A full catalogue record for this book is available from the British Library.

Acknowledgements
The publishers would like to thank the following for permission to reproduce photographs: Alamy p.22; Alamy/BtrandX Pictures/Steven Allen; Alamy/Imagestate p.4; Alamy/Science Photos p.18; CORBIS pp.19, 48, 51/Jerry Cooke; Find Photo p. 44; Fraser Photos p.6; Getty p.12; Harcourt Index pp.14, 21; NHPA/Polunin p.46; Peter Gould p.13; Photodisc/Getty Images p.5; Science Photo Library pp.11, 23, 27, 40; SPL/Eye of Science p.42; SPL/Georgia p.29; SPL/Madeley p.39; SPL/Pasieka p.20; SPL/Slawik p.32; Still Pictures p.34; Still Pictures/Brandon p.17; Stockfile/Steve Behr p.26; Trip p.52.

Cover photograph courtesy by Ed Bohon. Reproduced by kind permission of Corbis.

Artwork by David Woodroffe pp.7, 10; Jeff Edwards p.34; Lionel Jeans p.24; The Maltings Partnership p.47; Mark Franklin pp.9, 37.

The publishers would like to thank Robert Snedden for his assistance in the preparation of this book.

Every effort has been made to contact copyright holders of any material reproduced in this book. Any omissions will be rectified in subsequent printings if notice is given to the publishers.

One of the most spectacular human achievements has been to create and control light. By using natural light from the Sun, Moon and stars, and artificial light from candles, gas and electricity, we can light every part of the day and night. But what is light, and why is it so important?

What is light?

Light is a form of energy that travels in waves. Unlike sound waves, light waves can travel through a **vacuum**. This is why light from objects millions of miles away in space can reach the Earth. Light waves travel in straight lines. They can be **reflected** (change direction as they bounce off a solid object) or **refracted** (change direction as they pass through different materials, and this means they change speeds as well). It is these properties of light that give it the characteristics we use every day – but may not often think about.

Day for night
Present-day cities are almost as busy at night as during the day – because using electricity we can create light.

The electromagnetic spectrum

The light we can see is part of a massive family of electromagnetic waves, the **electromagnetic spectrum**. They all have different wavelengths, and this affects how they behave. The visible **spectrum** – the light we can actually see – is a very tiny part of the whole electromagnetic spectrum, which goes from radio waves at one end to gamma rays at the other. The wavelengh of **visble light** ranges from 400 to 700 nanometres. A nanometre is one thousand millionth of a metre.

Sensing light

What is happening in the room around you? Using your eyes you can see what is going on, and look at this book. Vision is one of the most important of the human senses, and we rely on it heavily. Human eyes are amazingly complicated organs for sensing light – and light is so important that most other organisms, plant and animal, are sensitive to it as well.

The human eye

Our eyes are remarkable and specialized organs. They are wonderfully adapted to enable us to be sensitive to the light that reaches us as it is scattered from everything around us. Our eyes allow us not only to see all the things in our surroundings, but also to be aware of what colour they are. Eyes are also an important part of who we are – the colour and shape of your eyes and the way your eyes and eyebrows move in response to what is happening around you, and in your interactions with others, make up a large part of your facial expressions. This in turn has a major impact on the way other people react to you.

Fly's eye
The eye of a fly is made up of thousands of tiny light-sensing units.

How the eye works

Light from objects around us enters our eyes through the **pupils**. The lens of the eye bends that light onto the **retina**, a light-sensitive layer at the back of the eyeball made up of special cells called **rods** and **cones**. Messages from the retina are transferred to the brain along the **optic nerve**. In the brain these messages are received and interpreted, giving us an image of the world around us.

The amount of light that comes into the eye is controlled by the **iris**, the coloured ring of muscle that surrounds the pupil. If the light is dim, the iris makes the pupil larger (it **dilates**) letting more light into the eye. If the light is very bright the pupil contracts to be very small, reducing the amount of light getting in to the eye so that it does not damage the retina.

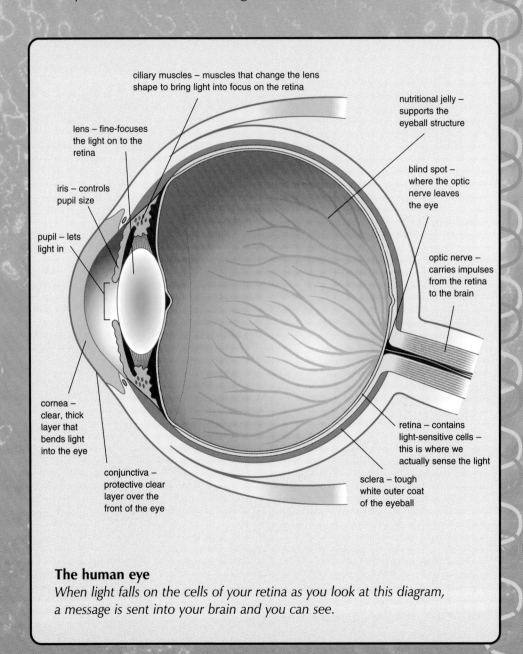

ciliary muscles – muscles that change the lens shape to bring light into focus on the retina

nutritional jelly – supports the eyeball structure

lens – fine-focuses the light on to the retina

blind spot – where the optic nerve leaves the eye

iris – controls pupil size

optic nerve – carries impulses from the retina to the brain

pupil – lets light in

cornea – clear, thick layer that bends light into the eye

retina – contains light-sensitive cells – this is where we actually sense the light

conjunctiva – protective clear layer over the front of the eye

sclera – tough white outer coat of the eyeball

The human eye
When light falls on the cells of your retina as you look at this diagram, a message is sent into your brain and you can see.

Fact or fantasy?

The ability to use the eyes to fool the brain is used in the making of films, such as the *Lord of the Rings* trilogy. The actor playing Gandalf the wizard is of normal height, and so are those playing the hobbits. Optical illusions are used to make us 'see' the hobbits as short and Gandalf as very tall. For example, scenes that showed the inside of hobbit holes used special effects with sloping floors and ceilings to make us believe Gandalf towered in a room that fitted Frodo Baggins to perfection.

Every sighted person relies heavily on what they can see – but how reliable are our senses? Our picture of the world depends partly on how our eyes work, and partly on how our brain interprets the information it receives from our eyes. Brains are enormously complex organs that take information from all our senses, to give each of us our own personal version of reality.

Upside-down images and blind spots

Because of the way the rays of light change direction as they pass through the lens of your eye, the image that forms on the retina of your eye is upside-down. However, you are never aware of this, because your brain has always seen it that way. In fact, if an image of an object is formed on your retina 'the right way up', you correctly perceive it to be actually upside-down!

Another clever trick of your brain is the way it deals with your **blind spot**. There is a patch on the back of your eye that is not sensitive to light, because this is where the optic nerve leaves the eyeball to go to the brain (see illustration on p.7). This means you have a blank patch, or 'blind spot' in what you can see. However, the brain uses the information from both eyes to fill in the blind spots for you. The only way you can find your blind spot is to trick your brain. Use the image across the page to have a go!

Find your own blind spots

Hold this page at arm's length. Close your left eye and stare hard at the cross with your right eye. You should be able to see both the cross and the spot. Now move the book slowly towards your face. At a certain point the spot should seem to disappear. This happens when the image of the spot falls on the blind spot of your right eye. Without information from the other eye, your brain fills in the blank with the same background as everything else it can see in that area. Often that would work, but in this case it does not! Reverse the instructions and try with the other eye, looking at the spot. This time it should be the cross that disappears.

Do you see?

✚   ●

Optical illusions

The brain is amazingly good at interpreting what we see, but sometimes the information we take in through our eyes fools our brain. **Optical illusions** are one example.

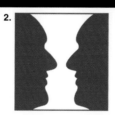

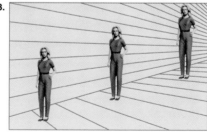

Fooled you!

What is happening in these optical illusions? Is it an old lady or a young girl (1), a goblet or two faces (2)? Who is really the tallest (3)? Illusions like these depend on confusion between the information coming in from your eyes and the usual way in which your brain interprets that information.

Bringing the world into focus

It is important not only that we are sensitive to light, but also that we can see clearly. The rays of light that arrive at our eyes **reflected** from objects near us are spreading out. This is different from the light rays reaching us from distant objects. They are travelling in almost parallel lines. The light coming in to your eye passes through the cornea, which bends it to pass through the pupil. The lens then adds some 'fine-tuning', so that the images you see are crisp and clear.

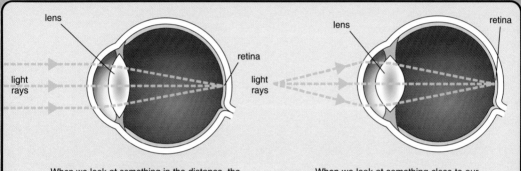

When we look at something in the distance, the light rays are nearly parallel. The lens is thin and flat because it does not need to bend the light rays much to focus them on to the retina.

When we look at something close to our eyes, the light rays are diverging. The lens needs to be thicker and fatter to bend the light rays into focus on the retina.

Sharp eyes
The change in shape of the lens of your eye allows you to bring light from both distant and close objects into focus on the back of the retina. This means that not only are you sensitive to light, you can also see clearly.

Failing to focus

Most young people can focus light equally well from things close to them and things in the distance. However, eyeball shape or the way the lens of the eye works means that some people have problems focusing either near or distant objects. In young people these problems are usually caused by the shape of the eye or the curve of the cornea. The most common problem is short-sightedness – things close by are clearly in focus, but distant objects appear rather fuzzy.

CATARACTS	
Age	Number affected per 1000 population
under 18	0.5
18–44	2.8
45–64	23.3
65–74	151.9
75+	198.6

Losing the light

As people and pets age, the lens of the eye can become cloudy, as dead tissue builds up inside it. This is called a cataract. Look through a piece of white tissue paper to get an idea of what it is like to have cataracts. Not enough light gets into the eye to see clearly, or in proper colour. Old people's (or dogs')

Gathering clouds
Cataracts are usually caused by accumulated damage in the lens of our eyes, and are closely linked to aging, as the chart shows. (Data, USA, late 1990s)

eyes often look milky – a sign of cataracts. Minor surgery solves this problem – the cataract is removed and replaced with an artificial lens.

In contrast, you may notice older people holding the newspaper further and further away from their eyes to read it clearly. They often become long-sighted – distant objects are easily seen but it becomes harder to focus closer up as the lens of the eye changes with age. Problems like these are easily solved using lenses to bend the light differently before it enters the eye. Glasses or contact lenses are worn by millions to correct problems in their vision. Increasingly, doctors are using another form of light – **lasers** – to restore perfect vision by operating on people to change the curve or the thickness of the cornea.

Lighting up our lives

There is one big problem with depending on light sensors to give us information about the world – for part of the day it is dark! When the Sun goes down, in primitive societies most activity stops. Although the human eye can adapt to the dim light given by the Moon and stars, to see in detail it needs bright light. So over the centuries people have developed better and better ways of providing artificial light. From candles and reed lights we have moved into the modern world, where electric lighting gives us the choice of working – and playing – long after the Sun goes down.

How light moves

Everybody has their own idea about how light behaves and what it is. Try asking any younger children you know – and perhaps the adults at home – and see what they say. Are their ideas about light the same as yours? It has taken many centuries for our modern ideas about light to be developed. The ancient Greeks thought that things could only be seen when they were touched by light rays given off by people's eyes. Since then all sorts of different theories have appeared, and in many cases disappeared again as they were shown to be wrong. In the next few pages we are going to explore some of our current knowledge about light and how it behaves.

Wave or particle?

Although we usually think of light as behaving like a wave, Albert Einstein showed that there are times when the only way to describe its behaviour is to think of it as particles or packets of energy. So physicists describe light as having **wave-particle duality** – and they choose to think of it either as a wave or as a particle, depending on what they are working on at the time. This is known as the **quantum theory**.

Straight rays at home

Light is a form of **energy**. It travels in waves, and these waves can pass through a **vacuum**, which is extremely important because it means light can reach us from the Sun and stars. Another important property of light becomes obvious when you use a torch. If you are moving around in the dark, and depending on the light from a torch, you cannot use your torch beam to see round corners. This is because light always travels in straight lines.

Hollywood skylight
When light beams sweep into the night sky, it is easy to see that light rays travel in straight lines.

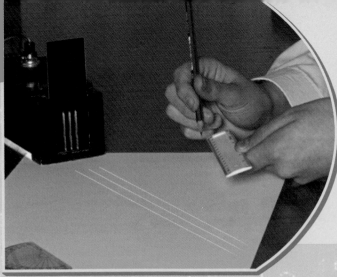

Light rays travelling in straight lines are all around us, but we don't notice them. The light box in this science lab allows us to demonstrate these light rays clearly.

Straight rays in the lab

The reason you can see objects that are miles away is also because light rays travel in straight lines. If they could curve, the light would wander all over the place and light from objects straight in front of you might never reach your eyes. Imagine travelling in a car at night if the light from the headlights curved around instead of shining straight on to the road – night-time travel would be impossible.

In the science lab there are many ways of demonstrating light rays and the ways in which they travel. Most of them involve putting grids or gratings in front of a source of light (known as a light box), so that straight beams of light can be seen.

Einstein – a true genius

Albert Einstein was born in Germany in 1879. He was a very mediocre student at school, and trained as a teacher before going on to become one of the greatest scientists the world has ever known. As well as producing his famous theory of relativity, he made huge contributions to our understanding of quantum theory, helping to explain the nature of light. He was awarded the Nobel Prize for Physics in 1921 for his work.

Whilst grappling with applying quantum theory to some of the apparently random behaviour of the Universe, he made the famous comment, 'God does not play dice with the Universe', summing up his deeply held view that everything could eventually be explained by science. In 1933 Einstein, who was Jewish, moved to the USA to escape Nazi persecution. He spent the rest of his life there.

The speed of light

Thunderstorms – some people are frightened of them, others find them exciting. Certainly, they are dramatic, powerful natural events. The brilliant flash of lightning is followed by the rumble and crash of thunder. Have you counted the seconds from the flash to the crash, to see how close the storm is? Why does counting this way locate the storm – and what do storms tell us about light?

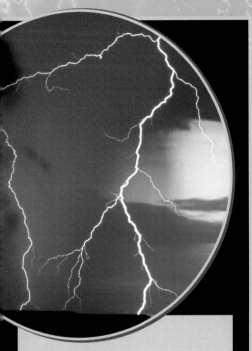

See it fast
Lightning reaches our eyes far faster than thunder reaches our ears, owing to the fantastic speed of light.

How fast is fast?

How fast does light really travel? The most accurate measurements put the speed of light at around 300,000 kilometres (186,420 miles) per second! Nothing in the Universe travels faster!

Lightning speed

The main thing storms show us is that light travels faster than sound. Lightning is a massive electrical spark earthing itself – travelling between the clouds and the ground. Lightning heats the air around it to a fantastic 30,000 °C, making the air expand so fast it breaks the sound barrier with the tremendous bang we call thunder. Lightning and thunder are actually almost simultaneous, but we see the lightning before we hear the thunder. This is because light travels much faster than sound. Light, at 299,792,458 metres per second, travels so fast that we see the lightning flash almost immediately. Sound travels at about 330 metres per second (depending on the temperature of the air), so the further away we are from the storm, the longer it takes for the sound of the thunder to reach us.

Finding the speed of light

Light travels far too fast to be measured using a normal clock, so for many centuries people had no real idea of its speed. In 1728, James Bradley made the first measurements of the speed of light using the position of the stars in the night sky. He was only 5 per cent out, but it was French physicist Hippolyte Fizeau who first had an idea that allowed him in 1849 to measure the speed of light with some accuracy. He shone a bright light from the top of a hill through gaps in a toothed wheel. The light bounced off a mirror on a hilltop 8 kilometres (5 miles) away, before returning to the wheel. Fizeau carried out complicated calculations by measuring the distance the wheel travelled, the speed it was rotating at and the distance the beam of light travelled.

Hippolyte Fizeau (1819-96)

Hippolyte Fizeau, who first measured the speed of light, was born in Paris. He inherited a fortune which enabled him to carry out the scientific research he loved. His interest in light developed from an original interest in photography. Fizeau later measured incredibly tiny distances, such as the amount moved when a crystal expands. Again he used the properties of light – in this case using the wavelength of light as the basis for his measurements.

His answer for the speed of light, 311,520 kilometres per second, was pretty close! Then, between 1926 and 1929 US scientist Albert Michelson performed some very similar experiments, using a rapidly turning mirror and another reflecting mirror 33.6 kilometres (21 miles) away. His results were much more accurate – but slow by 18 kilometres (11 miles) per second. Our modern measure for the speed of light has been achieved simply by refining these old methods, and using more accurate instruments.

Object	Speed
snail	0.05 km/h (0.03 mph)
human	24 km/h (15 mph)
cheetah (fastest land animal)	96 km/h (60 mph)
fastest train	515 km/h (320 mph)
fastest car (land speed record)	1227 km/h (763 mph)
sound	1234.8 km/h (767.3mph)
jet aircraft	3529 km/h (2192 mph)
space shuttle	28,000 km/h (17,500mph)
light	1,080,000,000 km/h (670,680,000 mph)

What a whiz
Compared to some everyday speeds, the speed of light seems even more impressive.

Bouncing light

Looking in the mirror is something most of us take for granted. We rely on being able to see a **reflected** image of ourselves to make us look presentable, or to admire ourselves. Archaeologists have found mirrors that were used in civilizations centuries old, because we have always had a fascination with looking at ourselves. Mirrors have all sorts of uses – but what is happening to the light when we look in a mirror?

Cool colours

Light-coloured surfaces reflect more light than dark-coloured surfaces. This is why a white car parked in the Sun will be cooler when you return to it than a black or dark blue car. Black clothing may be 'cool' for the fashion-conscious, but white clothing will keep you cooler on a sunny day! In the same way, the black polythene sheets used by gardeners absorb light energy from the Sun and warm up the soil. Shiny surfaces, whatever colour they are, will reflect more light than matt or non-shiny surfaces. This is why matt black surfaces are used in solar heating panels, to absorb as much light energy as possible.

Reflection

A smooth, flat, shiny surface can make a ray of light change direction. When a ray of light hits a shiny surface it is bounced, or reflected, back. The mirrors we use every day are made up of a shiny reflective surface protected by a sheet of glass. If a mirror or other reflective surface is very smooth, the light will be bounced off it cleanly to give a reflected image – what we call a reflection, when we look in the mirror. On a smooth mirror surface, the angle at which the light will be bounced off will be the same as the one at which it hit the mirror. If the surface is shiny but not smooth, the light will be reflected back at all sorts of unpredictable angles, so it will not produce a clear image.

Alaskan lake, Chugach mountains

Reflections are always formed by light bouncing off a shiny solid or a liquid surface, like this lake.

Other materials that are not mirrors can also reflect light, and they play an important part in our everyday life. For example, the road signs that show up as the car headlights hit them, and the reflective material used on bags and clothing to help make us visible to cars at night; both help to make our roads safer to use. The cats' eyes that mark out major roads also rely on reflecting back the light from headlights to become visible.

Driving in the dark can also show us another example of reflection, when the eyes of a cat or other nocturnal animal glow back at us when they are caught in the car headlights. Reflective material on the back of their eyeballs designed to capture and make use of low light levels, reflects back the glare of the headlights and makes the eyes of the animal brilliantly visible.

Did you know?

A sheet of glass reflects about 5% of the light that falls on it – the rest passes straight through. With darkness on one side and light on the other, anyone on the bright side can see their reflection in the glass. But anyone on the dark side can see everything on the light side. Remember that on winter evenings when the curtains are not drawn!

How light is shaped

Poke a straw into a glass of water and look at it. It will look different under the water, as if it is bent – but it is not the straw, but the light itself that is bent! As a ray of light passes from one material to another it is bent, or **refracted**.

Bending light

Why? Light travels at different speeds in different materials, and this is what makes it bend. Try using this model to help you understand. Picture a row of children running in a straight line, all at the same speed, diagonally across a beach into the sea. Some of the children will be running through the water while others are still on the sand. The children in the water will slow down, because it is harder to run in water – and so the line will bend. Light waves behave like this. A light ray bends where it enters water, or glass, or plastic.

Liquid bender
*This ruler looks like it is broken in two pieces, but this is an **optical illusion** caused by light refracting.*

Lenses

The way light bends as it passes through different materials explains what lenses do. When we looked at the way our eyes work, we saw that both the cornea and the lens bend light to bring it into focus on our **retina**. Now we can see exactly how this is done. The stuff the cornea is made of, the thickness of it and the curve, mean that the light passing through it is all bent towards the **pupil** of the eye. Then by changing the shape of the lens, making it fatter or thinner, our eye can change the amount the light is bent, to make sure it ends up in focus on the retina.

The same applies to the lenses we use to correct vision problems. The shape and thickness of the lens affects how the light is bent before it reaches our eyes.

Sunny days, heat haze

Travellers in deserts know about the dangers of mirages – pools of water appearing to people who are frantic with thirst. We may never visit the desert, but we have 'mirages' much closer to home. On hot summer days, the surface of the road can appear to shimmer – as if there is water on the road.

Common sense tells us it is not, but our eyes insist it is there. This is yet another example of refraction. The road, being dark, absorbs light and heat and becomes very hot, as does the air just above it. As the hot air rises, it cools. Hot air is less dense than cooler air, so light travels faster in the hot air than in the cooler air. A ray of light from the sky is bent as it passes from the cool air into the hotter air near the surface of the road and back into cooler air again. Rays of light from the sky reach our eyes from the road – so we see a patch of 'sky' on the road. Our brains interpret the light, shiny patch as 'water', because it makes more sense than 'sky'! As we move closer, the angles change and the image disappears.

Refraction in action!

Heat haze mirages on roads in hot weather are caused by the refraction of light travelling through air at different temperatures.

Splitting light

Imagine a sudden, sharp shower on a beautiful sunny day. The Sun keeps shining even though it is pouring – and overhead appears a rainbow, a massive arc of colour in the sky. Rainbows always seem special. As children we may have been told that there is a pot of gold at the end of a rainbow – it is only as we grow up that we realize that there is no pot of gold, because rainbows have no end. In fact, the explanation for the beautiful colours is firmly rooted in science. We can even make our own 'mini-rainbows' in the lab or at home.

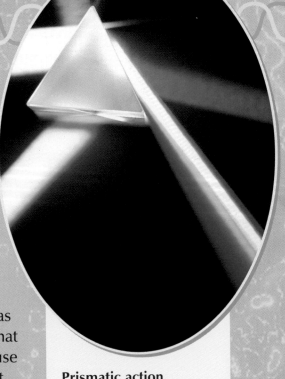

Prismatic action
White light reveals its true colours – the spectrum of light from red to violet can be seen clearly using a prism – or a diamond!

White light, coloured light

The light we see is called **white light** or visible light. It is actually made up of light of all the different colours, combined together. White light can be split up, back into its different colours, using **dispersion**. This is a process in which the light is passed through a special piece of glass called a **prism**, producing a **spectrum** of all the different colours. Each colour of light has a different wavelength – red light has the longest wavelength and blue light the shortest – and they travel at different speeds in water and in glass. This is how a prism works, as each colour is refracted by a different amount and bends at a different angle. Red bends the least and violet the most. The result is the spectrum of colours that delights us in the rainbow, and that is also lovely when formed on a smaller scale with the prism. The order of the colours is red, orange, yellow, green, blue, indigo and violet. In a rainbow, each tiny droplet of water acts as a prism, splitting the sunlight into the spectrum that we see arcing across the sky.

The different colours of light that we can see belong to a much larger family of waves, most of which we cannot see – they are part of the **electromagnetic spectrum**. This electromagnetic spectrum touches almost every aspect of our lives, from domestic appliances to life-saving medical treatments. As well as visible light it includes radio waves, microwaves, infrared light, **ultraviolet** light, X-rays and gamma rays.

Full-spectrum living

We use almost the whole electromagnetic spectrum one way or another in our electrical goods – these are examples you probably have at home.

Seeing colour

What's your favourite colour? We don't see the world in black and white – we see it in an enormous range of colours, and colours are very important to us. The light that hits the world is white light from the Sun. Different coloured objects absorb different wavelengths of light – and what they do not absorb, they **reflect** back.

We have three different types of **cone** cells on our retinas, which respond to the three primary colours of light – red, blue and green. Mixtures of these three colours of light give us all the colours we can see. (The primary colours of light are different from paint primary colours – mix red, blue and green paints together you get a sludgy brown!)

So for example, something that absorbs red and blue light will reflect green light back. This will be picked up by our green-sensitive cones, and we will see that object as green. Any object that reflects back almost all the light that hits it will appear white, while objects that absorb almost all light will appear black.

Filtering it out

White light is wonderful stuff, but we do not always want white light. Think of traffic lights, indicator and brake lights on cars, atmospheric coloured lights on stage and in restaurants, red warning lights and blue flashing emergency lights. Although the light produced by the light bulbs used in all these cases is white light, using coloured filters or glass allows us to change the colour of the light we see.

How do filters work?

When you use filters in science lessons to separate mixtures of substances, the filters allow some things to pass through but not others. Light filters work in a similar way – only some colours of light can pass through, the others are absorbed by the filter. In traffic lights, a red filter absorbs all the colours of light except red – so only red light gets through and that is what we see. In the same way, the green traffic light has a filter that absorbs all the colours except green – so we see a green light.

Magical colours
These lights depend on coloured glass as filters. Each tiny filament produces white light, but only some colours can pass through the glass.

Changing colour

We can filter out some of the colours of white light to give us whatever colour we choose. But the colour we see will depend not only on the filter we have used, but also on what we shine the light on to.

This red ball is under a white light. Its red colour is caused by its reflection of the red light within the white light.

Here the red ball is under a red light. Again, it appears red.

The red ball here is under a green light. It appears black because it absorbs, rather than reflects, the green light.

Now you see it
Bouncing light makes this red ball appear differently coloured, depending on the colour of the light source.

White surfaces are the best for showing up the true colour of a light. They reflect back all the light that hits them, so a red light shone on to white paper will appear red, and a green light shone on to white paper will appear green. A red light shone on to red paper will also appear red, because the paper is absorbing all colours except red and reflecting red light. However, if you shine a red light on to green paper it will look black, because green paper absorbs all colours of light except green. All the red light is absorbed, so no light at all is reflected back to your eyes. This means that the area where the red light is shining will appear black.

The light we get from light bulbs in our homes or from the lighting in shops is not the same as light from the Sun. Ordinary light bulbs usually produce light that is quite yellow in tone, while fluorescent lights produce light containing more blue. This is why we have to be really careful matching colours in shops, because of the different colour tones in the artificial lights and the fabrics. A perfect match in the shop can look really odd out in the sunlight!

Making use of light

There are probably plenty of photographs on display in your home. Newspapers and magazines are full of photos, too, each capturing an important moment. Photos record major events in our lives, and world events around us. They are taken using cameras, machines that use light to record an image.

How do cameras work?

There are many different types of camera, from the simple **pinhole camera** that you can make at home, to the most sophisticated professional camera with a multitude of lenses, but they all work on the same basic principles. There are many similarities between a camera and the human eye. However, whereas the **retina** is the light-sensitive part of the eye, the light sensitivity of the camera is provided by the film.

All conventional cameras work by focusing the right amount of light on to a light-sensitive film to form an image. The amount of light allowed in can be changed by adjusting the size of the aperture, that is, the hole through which light enters the camera. The exposure time can be changed by varying the amount of time the aperture stays open.

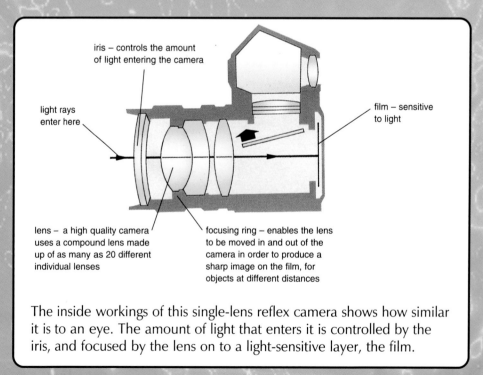

iris – controls the amount of light entering the camera

light rays enter here

film – sensitive to light

lens – a high quality camera uses a compound lens made up of as many as 20 different individual lenses

focusing ring – enables the lens to be moved in and out of the camera in order to produce a sharp image on the film, for objects at different distances

The inside workings of this single-lens reflex camera shows how similar it is to an eye. The amount of light that enters it is controlled by the iris, and focused by the lens on to a light-sensitive layer, the film.

A brief history of photography

1816 The first photograph is taken by the Frenchman Joseph Nicéphore Niepce. He photographed the view from his window, exposing the film for eight hours.

1839 The first photograph of a person is taken by Louis Daguerre, who developed a much more sensitive film that needed exposing for under a minute. The first commercially manufactured camera went on sale in the same year.

1840 William Fox-Talbot invents the positive–negative process that meant copies could be made of photographs. Before this each photo was a 'one-off'.

1861 The first colour photograph is taken by James Clerk Maxwell.

1888 The Kodak company, selling affordable box cameras and rolls of film, is formed by George Eastman.

1948 The Polaroid instant camera, invented by Edwin Herbert Land, arrives on the market.

1990s The digital camera, converting light information into digital signals for use with a computer, is developed and marketed.

The light-sensitive film is vitally important to the whole process of photography with a conventional camera. This is how it is made, and how it works. A thin plastic film is coated with a chemical – normally a silver compound. When light falls on this chemical, a reaction called **photochemical decomposition** takes place, producing silver metal on the film. Where more light falls on a bit of film, there will be more silver. This forms a negative image – the light areas appear dark (large amounts of silver) while the darker areas appear light. The negative can then be used to make a positive image – a photograph – by shining light through it onto another piece of photographic emulsion. In a digital camera there is no film. The image is focused onto a microchip that captures the image. The image can then be down-loaded into a compter and printed off.

Colour photographs work on the same principle as black and white, except the film is made up of three layers, each containing different chemicals. One is sensitive to blue light, one to green and one to red. When the film is processed, yellow, magenta and cyan (bright turquoise) dyes are added to the layers to give a full-colour image.

More uses of light

What was the last film you saw at the cinema? Do you have home videos or DVDs? Almost everybody uses and enjoys these developments of the light-sensitive camera – capable of recording image after image on film that can then be played back fast enough for the human eye to see them as a moving image. The human eye can only see the separate images if they pass the eye relatively slowly. Once they are moving at more than 23 images per second we see continuous movement.

CDs and DVDs

The information stored on CDs and DVDs is retrieved using red light. The surface of the disc **reflects** light, except where tiny pits are burnt into it during recording. These absorb red light. In the player red light is beamed onto the disc at an angle and reflected to a sensor, except where there are pits. The presence or absence of reflected red light gives a digital signal (either on or off) which is then converted to an electrical signal and then into sound or pictures.

Alarm systems

We regularly use light in alarm systems. Banks, businesses and museums all use alarm systems. Burglar alarms are installed in our homes, too. Alarm systems designed to detect intruders often use a beam of light – they are photo-sensors. They have two main components: a source of focused light, either a **laser** beam or infrared light, and a light sensor.

Visual warning
When light sensors inside the house have been triggered, setting off the alarm, a light comes on outside the house to alert people.

Thomas Edison, the US inventor of light bulbs, sued British inventor Swan when he found Swan had made a light bulb like his. He was unsuccessful, because Swan was really first. He had made the first successful electric light bulb – but had not patented his invention because he thought people would copy it anyway.

Edison and Swan
The story of Edison (above) and Swan's rivalry has a happy ending; once the dust had settled they joined forces to form a company making light bulbs!

In the simplest kind of home security system, you aim the beam at the light sensor, often across a passageway. When somebody walks between the light source and the sensor, the path of the beam is blocked briefly. The sensor registers a drop in light levels and sends a signal to the control box. More sophisticated systems have passive infrared (PIR) detectors. These sensors 'see' the infrared **energy** emitted by the warm body of an intruder. They can be used inside or outside. They detect a sharp increase in infrared energy, and set off an alarm in the house or turn on outside security lights. PIR detectors used in household burglar alarm systems are designed to trigger the alarm only when infrared energy levels change very rapidly, to avoid false alarms due to normal changes in infrared emissions caused by heating the house. If these sensors are triggered once the alarm has been set, the alarms will sound, alerting neighbours and the police that something is wrong.

Speed traps

Unfortunately many people think they do not need to keep to the speed limits imposed on the roads. This is a major cause of accidents. To save lives, the police have developed a whole range of 'speed traps' – devices for measuring the speeds of motorists and recording who is travelling too fast.

Catching offenders

Speed cameras and speed guns are a familiar sight on our roads. Many involve radar – using radio waves that are part of the **electromagnetic spectrum** – linked to ordinary flash cameras that provide the light to take photographs of offenders. However, the most recent technology uses a different kind of light – infrared light – to trap speeding motorists. The lidar (light detecting and ranging) gun measures the time it takes a burst of highly focused infrared light to reach a car, bounce off and return to its starting point. By multiplying this time by the speed of light, the lidar system determines how far away the car is. The system sends out many of these infrared bursts in a short period, to collect a series of measurements of the car. It uses these measurements to calculate how fast the car is moving. Lidar guns may take several hundred samples in less than half a second, so they are extremely accurate. Once they detect someone speeding, they automatically record the speed of the car and take a photo that shows the car registration and the person driving.

Light traps
When cars travel too fast, more accidents occur and more people are killed. That is why the police are always looking for new ways of catching people who are speeding. The lidar system uses light to fight crime and save lives.

Age of drivers involved	% of fatal accidents caused by excess speed	% of injury accidents caused by excess speed
15–19	40.5	19.1
20–24	25.0	15.0
25–29	17.6	10.9
30–39	13.6	7.7
40–59	12.3	4.1
60+	8.2	2.5

Lasers - lighting the way

Laser lights are a familiar sight at rock concerts and on TV spectaculars. They are also commonly used in a much more boring context, at the supermarket checkout for reading the barcodes on our shopping. Everything has its own barcode, and simply passing the laser decoder over it enables the till to register what the purchase is and how much it costs.

The number of uses people are finding for lasers is growing all the time. They are used for delicate surgery – where they seal the wound and prevent bleeding as they cut – yet they are also used in factories to cut thick steel sheets. They travel in very precise parallel lines so they are used for surveying, and they are used to create holograms, 3-D images that can be used both for fun and in industry.

Light stick

Laser light is a beam of very focused, 'concentrated' light. Laser stands for Light Amplification by Stimulated Emission of Radiation. Electricity is used to excite the **electrons** in the solid, liquid or gas that is being used to produce the laser light.

This produces a beam of very regular light waves, all moving in the same direction. The colour of the laser light depends on the elements present in the laser material – for example a helium–neon laser emits red light.

Communicating using light

Ever since people have used boats at sea, they have been at risk of crashing onto rocks hidden below the surface of the water. Wherever there are boats at sea today, on special buoys and ships and along every coastline in lighthouses, warning lights are used to communicate with sailors, informing them of the dangers of rocks, hidden shallows and dangerous currents. Lighthouses are a form of digital communication – the signal is either on or off.

Using light to talk

Wherever you live, you can be in touch with other people. Thanks to modern technology, you can talk to people in the same town, hundreds of miles away or even in another country or continent. We all use the telephone so frequently that we tend to take it for granted, but it is an amazing piece of technology. What is more, increasing numbers of land-based phones turn our voices into patterns of light travelling across the world at mind-boggling speed. The input of our voices into the phone is converted into an electrical signal, which in turn is converted into pulses of light. This is known as a digital signal – there either is a pulse, or there is not, so it is either on or off.

Some systems use ordinary light, others use infrared light. These light pulses travel along **optical fibres**, and on reaching their destination are converted back into the sounds we hear as we listen to someone talking on the phone. Hundreds, and even thousands of messages can travel along the same fibre at the same time, at the speed of light.

How optical fibres work

Optical fibres are very thin solid fibres – thinner than a human hair – made of glass. Because the fibre is so thin, the light travelling along it keeps meeting the edges of the fibres at a very shallow angle. This means that all of the light is reflected back into the fibre and keeps travelling along it. Because the light simply bounces off the walls of the fibre, none of it is lost – in fact, optical fibres are sometimes referred to as light pipes. The fibre must be thin enough to make the light bounce off its walls instead of travelling straight through them, and the fibres must not be bent too sharply or they may be damaged.

Take a look inside

Optical fibres are used in a medical instrument called an endoscope. This is a bundle of optical fibres with a tiny camera attached. Doctors pass it down the throat into a patient's stomach. The light which passes along the fibres enables them to see clearly inside the body without cutting the patient open, so they can diagnose conditions such as stomach ulcers and cancer more easily, economically and with less risk to the patient.

Optical fibre lamps
In a lamp made from simple optical fibres, the only light you can see is the light that escapes from the end of each fibre. The fine points of bobbing light create a dazzling effect.

Light and dark through the year

Imagine being outside on a clear night, away from the lights of town and city, looking up into the sky. What can you see? The biggest and most obvious object in the sky at night is the Moon. Keep looking – as your eyes adjust to the dim light you will see more and more planets and stars, some so dim that they are on the very edge of vision. The number of stars in the night sky can be almost overwhelming.

What is moonlight?

The glare of street lights and cars prevents city-dwellers from noticing how bright moonlight can be. When the Moon is full, the moonlight can be so bright that the whole countryside is bathed in a soft, silver glow. Familiar objects are visible and even have 'moon-**shadows**'. This light is not really moonlight at all, because the Moon is a rocky satellite of the Earth, producing no light of its own. Moonlight is simply a **reflection** of the Sun's light shining onto the Moon.

Moon phases
When the side of the Moon that we see is dark – around a new moon – the far side of the Moon is in sunlight and very little is reflected back to Earth. A full moon occurs when the side of the Moon facing the Earth is in sunshine – and the light is reflected back to the Earth.

What about the stars?

For thousands of years, people just like you have gazed at the night sky and tried to make sense of what they saw. Now people have walked on the surface of the Moon, we have the use of immensely powerful telescopes to help us see the light from distant stars and we have sent out probes to the other planets in our solar system. Our knowledge of the stars is greater now than at any time in recorded human history.

Our nearest star is the Sun. It is a massive ball of immensely hot gases, where nuclear reactions are constantly taking place – the temperature of the centre ends up at about 15,000,000 °C. Vast amounts of **energy** are released – about four million tonnes of mass are lost every second, and this is converted into 386 billion billion megawatts of energy, much of which is radiated as heat, light and gamma rays. (Compare this to the Earth – the average production of one of our power stations is only around 2000 megawatts per year.)

This is the source of the light reaching Earth. The distance between the Sun and Earth is so great that the light from the Sun takes some time to reach us. If the Sun went out now – it would be eight minutes before we were plunged into total darkness and cold.

A sky full of suns

The stars we see in the night sky are objects like our Sun – millions and billions of Suns, unimaginable miles away. The light from the stars travels so far to reach our eyes and our telescopes that when we see a really distant star the light reaching our eyes left the star a very long time ago. We are not actually seeing the star as it is now – we are looking at events that happened hundreds, thousands or even millions of years ago – an awe-inspiring thought.

Measuring distance in light years

A **light year** is the distance that light can travel in a year – a distance almost too big to get our heads around. For example, our nearest star after the Sun is called Proxima Centauri. It is 4.2 light years away – a small distance of 40,000 billion kilometres!

Day and night

The Sun is at the centre of our solar system, and the Earth travels around the Sun in an orbit that takes one year. At the same time it is spinning around every 24 hours on its axis, an imaginary line joining the North and South poles. This rotation makes it look as if the Sun is moving across the sky. You will not have noticed a spinning sensation, but you are actually travelling at about 1670 kilometres (1038 miles) per hour if you are standing on the equator.

Spinning Earth

Wherever you live on the globe, for part of every 24 hours you are facing the Sun. The light from the Sun reaches you, and it is then daytime. As the Earth continues to spin, the part where you are turns away from the Sun, you lose the light and day turns into night.

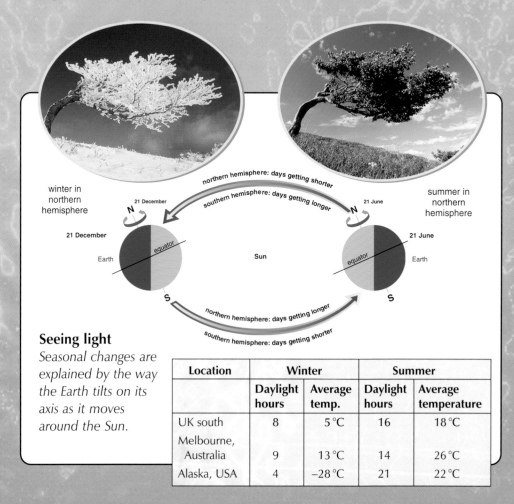

winter in northern hemisphere

21 December

northern hemisphere: days getting shorter

southern hemisphere: days getting longer

21 June

summer in northern hemisphere

21 December

Earth

equator

Sun

equator

21 June

Earth

northern hemisphere: days getting longer

southern hemisphere: days getting shorter

Seeing light

Seasonal changes are explained by the way the Earth tilts on its axis as it moves around the Sun.

Location	Winter		Summer	
	Daylight hours	Average temp.	Daylight hours	Average temperature
UK south	8	5 °C	16	18 °C
Melbourne, Australia	9	13 °C	14	26 °C
Alaska, USA	4	−28 °C	21	22 °C

The seasons of the year

As the spinning of the Earth on its axis gives us our 24-hour day, so the Earth's yearly orbiting of the Sun gives us the seasons – but how? The Earth leans on its axis at an angle of 23.5° to the vertical. When the Earth is on one side of the Sun, the northern hemisphere is tilted towards the Sun. The Sun rises high in the sky and the days are long and hot. It is summer in the northern hemisphere and winter in the south. Six months later, when the Earth is on the other side of the Sun, the situation is reversed – the northern hemisphere is tilted away from the Sun and so the Sun appears lower in the sky and the days are shorter – it is winter. Whichever hemisphere is leaning towards the Sun receives more of the Sun's energy. Spring and autumn are the transitional stages with equal amounts of daylight and darkness, as the Earth moves from one extreme to the other.

Changing the seasons

Around the equator the daylight hours and temperature vary little during the year. In many parts of the world, though, the changes in daylight hours that come with the changing seasons have a major effect on the time at which animals have their young and on the flowering and fruiting of plants. This is why each season has its own displays of flowers. But we often like to have flowers in our homes at the 'wrong' time of year – poinsettias at Christmas, roses for Valentine's day – and so specialist plant growers have learnt to 'change the seasons' for plants grown in greenhouses. By altering the amount of light the plants receive – for example, blocking out summer daylight then lengthening winter days using special lighting – growers can fool plants into responding as if it is their flowering season at almost any time of year.

SAD without light

The pure **white light** of daylight seems to be important for human health and mental well-being. In countries where the days become much shorter in the winter, people have far less daylight exposure, particularly if they work in an office. Seasonal affective disorder (SAD) is a type of depression linked to lack of daylight in winter. Sufferers can improve their condition by using a light box that gives out daylight-simulating white light for an hour or two each day.

The world of shadows

Most of us have played with shadows – making images on the wall with the shadows of our hands, or using shadow puppets. Why are shadows formed?

Sharp or fuzzy?

Light rays travel in straight lines and cannot bend round **opaque** objects. Therefore no light falls on the surface behind an opaque object – in marked contrast to the area around it, where light does fall. This darkened region is what we call a shadow.

Shadow play

Shadows have long been used for entertainment – who has not made a rabbit or a duck's head on the wall with the shadow of their hand? In many parts of the world, such as China, India and Thailand, full shadow theatres are very popular. The puppets perform behind an illuminated screen while the audience watches the shadows. In India these shadow plays can continue for weeks!

Shadows can be clear and crisp with sharp edges, or much fuzzier, depending on the light source. A small, concentrated light source casts sharp, clear shadows while a large, spread-out light source makes big, fuzzy shadows. You can see the difference using a torch and a small object at home. Hold the object close to the torch, where the beam is tight, and then much further away, and compare the shadows.

Umbra and penumbra

Most of the shadows we see by day are cast by the Sun. Animals rely on shadows for shelter, and often their coat patterns mimic the patterns of light and shade in their natural environment. When the Sun is directly overhead at midday it casts no shadow. However, when it is rising or setting, the shadows it produces are long – much longer than the objects producing them. All the shadows of objects on Earth produced by the Sun have clear, crisp edges because they are so small compared to the Sun that the rays of light arriving from the Sun are effectively parallel. However, in shadows produced by artificial light (where the light rays are spreading out) we can sometimes see two parts to the shadow, the **umbra** (the darkest part) and the **penumbra** (the less dark part).

Eclipse!

One of the most dramatic examples of shadows in the natural world is something most of us will see only once or twice – a **solar eclipse**. During an eclipse of the Sun, the Moon passes directly between the Earth and the Sun, so that its shadow falls on one area of the Earth's surface. The Moon is so huge that even with sunlight there is an umbra and a penumbra. The shadow's penumbra gives a partial eclipse, where dusk falls even though it is daytime. Sometimes only the penumbra falls on the Earth, giving a partial eclipse only. When and where the umbra falls on the Earth, there is a total eclipse. The Sun disappears completely for a few minutes, the Earth becomes as dark as night and the air feels cold. It is not surprising that our ancestors centuries ago thought that a monster had swallowed the Sun, and panicked in case the Sun never appeared again!

In a **lunar eclipse** the Earth passes between the Sun and the Moon, so that the shadow of the Earth moves across the face of the Moon, eventually covering it completely. Although not so dramatic as a solar eclipse, a lunar eclipse lasts much longer – the Moon turns a dim orange-brown colour for an hour or so, as it is lit only by sunlight **refracted** round the Earth by the atmosphere.

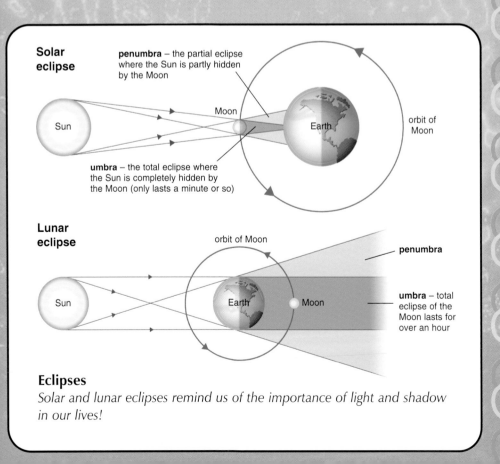

Solar eclipse

penumbra – the partial eclipse where the Sun is partly hidden by the Moon

Sun

Moon

Earth

orbit of Moon

umbra – the total eclipse where the Sun is completely hidden by the Moon (only lasts a minute or so)

Lunar eclipse

orbit of Moon

penumbra

Sun

Earth

Moon

umbra – total eclipse of the Moon lasts for over an hour

Eclipses

Solar and lunar eclipses remind us of the importance of light and shadow in our lives!

Colours in the sky

Light from the Sun sets the pattern of our days and nights, even with readily available artificial light. The Moon and the stars brighten the night sky. But there are other natural light displays in the sky, and they make up some of the most spectacular and colourful light phenomena of all.

Rainbow colours

The sight of a rainbow arching across the sky, with the colours of the **spectrum** tinting everything we see through them, is something we all enjoy. We only see rainbows when a special set of conditions is in place. The Sun must be shining from behind you while at the same time it is raining in front of you. When the **white light** from the Sun travels through the individual drops of water, the different colours of light are bent differently. As a result of this **diffraction**, the light is split into the colours of the spectrum and a rainbow appears. When we see a rainbow as we look up from the Earth, it appears as an arc in the sky, but actually what we see is part of a complete circle. Sometimes, lucky aircraft passengers are able to see the whole thing!

Why is the sky blue?

Rainbows, although beautiful, do not appear every day. But every clear day we see a blue sky – and often the most wonderful shades of pink, orange, gold, red and even violet and green, as the Sun rises and sets. Where do these colours come from?

The atmosphere of the Earth is made up of molecules of several different gases. These molecules scatter the light from the Sun as it passes through them. Blue light is scattered more than red light. We cannot look directly at the Sun, which means that most of the light which reaches our eyes consists of blue light which has been scattered by the atmosphere, and so the sky looks blue. However, as the Sun first emerges above the horizon at dawn, and when it sinks down again at sunset, the light has to travel through more of the atmosphere. The blue light gets scattered so much that only the red, orange and yellow reaches us – so the sky gets its glorious colours.

The auroras

The most spectacular light show on Earth can sometimes be seen by people in northern parts of North America, in some of the Northern European countries, such as Greenland, and in southern lands such as Australia.

These lights are the famous *Aurora borealis* (the Northern Lights) and the *Aurora australis* (the Southern Lights). These dramatic flickering patterns and curtains of light appear in the night sky throughout the winter months. Charged particles from space, emitted millions of miles away by the Sun, stream into the Earth's atmosphere, attracted by the magnetic poles at the north and south of the planet. As these charged particles hit gas particles in the atmosphere, coloured light is radiated in wonderful swirling patterns.

Aurora borealis, Manitoba, Canada
Lights arising from the impact of streams of particles from space form sweeping, moving patterns in the sky.

Letting light through

Look out of the window – what can you see? Whatever it is, you can see it because the material in the window – glass or plastic – is **transparent**. This means that almost all the light that falls on that material is transmitted right through it to the other side, where it can enter your eyes. Everyday materials respond to light in several ways. Transparent materials are used when we need to see through things. They form little or no **shadow** as light travels through them.

Just passing through

Many other materials are **translucent**. This means that although light is transmitted through the material, some of it is absorbed. The light entering the material is scattered in all directions by the particles that make up the material, so you cannot see clearly through the material, which appears milky. Many plastics are translucent, and so is your skin, and many, many other everyday things.

Finally, many materials are **opaque**. They do not allow any light to travel through them – they either **reflect** the light back, or absorb it.

Isaac Newton
Newton (1642–1727) is considered the 'father' of physics. Amongst his many discoveries was the make-up of white light.

Who's who of light

Our knowledge about the nature of light and how it works has been built up over many years. Here are just some of the people who have helped to develop our understanding of light:

1665 onwards The outstanding British scientist Sir Isaac Newton began to make his series of discoveries about light, the first being that white light can be split into a spectrum of seven colours by a **prism**. Many of his discoveries were about optics – he also spent a lot of time arguing about it with other scientists who had different ideas. He did not publish his results until 1704.

1728/9 British astronomer James Bradley came up with the first reasonably accurate measurement of the speed of light – he was only five per cent out!

1803 Another British scientist, Thomas Young, proved that light takes the form of waves. His experiments showed that light waves interfere with each other just as water waves do.

1849 Hippolyte Fizeau achieved a fairly accurate measure of the speed of light using his toothed wheel.

February 1879 British inventor Joseph Swan invented the electric light bulb, using a carbon filament.

December 1879 American inventor Thomas Edison invented the electric light bulb, using a carbon filament.

1880s Swan and Edison worked together to manufacture light bulbs.

1901 German physicist Max Planck suggested that light might exist both as a particle and as a wave.

1926–29 American Albert Michelson improved the accuracy of the measurement of the speed of light for the first time in nearly 200 years.

Light in the living world

Look around you – there is probably a plant not far away. Plants come in all shapes and sizes, from the microscopic to the largest trees. We grow plants for food and for their beauty. The greens of their foliage are soothing and the colours of their flowers appealing – but what we are perhaps less aware of is that plants, and their relationship to light, are vital for the whole of life on Earth.

Light makes food

Plants are mainly green, and this is because they contain **chlorophyll**, a green pigment that has one very special property. It captures light **energy** so that it can be used by the cells of the plant to make food.

Light from the Sun powers down on the surface of the Earth all the time. It keeps us warm and enables us to see. More than this, through the amazing biochemistry of plants, it also provides us with oxygen to breathe and food to eat, and removes the carbon dioxide we produce as waste.

Agave leaf
Chlorophyll, which captures light, is stored in chloroplasts (the green balls in the picture) found in leaf cells. These cells are light-powered sugar-making chemical factories.

Light power

Around 10^{19} kilojoules of solar energy is used each year in photosynthesis to convert carbon dioxide into biological material in plants. This light-driven energy flow through living plants is around twenty times greater than the energy flow through all the machines that people have created in the world.

In the leaves of every plant is a complex chemical factory making sugar, and the single most important reaction involves light. The light is trapped by the chlorophyll and used to make a special high-energy chemical called ATP. This ATP is then used to provide the energy to join together molecules of water (from the soil) and carbon dioxide (from the air) to make a simple sugar. What is more, the waste product of this reaction is oxygen, which is then released back into the air. The whole process is called **photosynthesis**.

The process of photosynthesis can be demonstrated like this:

carbon dioxide + water + light energy → sugar + oxygen

Feeding the world

Light energy powers photosynthesis and this means that, effectively, light feeds the world.

This might seem a bit of an overstatement – light certainly enables plants to make food for themselves, but does it really feed the world? The simple answer is 'yes'. Plants make food during photosynthesis powered by light. People and animals eat plants. People and animals also eat animals that have eaten plants. Almost every type of living organism on the Earth depends on light as the ultimate source of its food.

Light matters

The importance of photosynthesis is shown by the number of Nobel prizes awarded to people who have helped work out exactly what happens when light hits plants. Here are just a few:

1915 German scientist Richard Willstätter won a Nobel prize after showing that chlorophyll plays an important part in photosynthesis.

1954 The American Melvin Calvin set up a team who worked out the reactions by which carbon dioxide is converted into sugars. He won a Nobel prize in 1961.

1960–61 Robert Hill and Fay Bendall in the UK, and Louis Duysens working quite independently in the Netherlands, showed the detailed role of light in photosynthesis – and all won Nobel prizes.

Patterns of life

Most children grow plants from seeds at some time, either at home or at school. A tray of seeds left on the windowsill for a few days will grow seedlings that lean over, bending their leaves towards the light. Plants are so dependent on light that they have a whole series of responses to both the level of light and the direction it is coming from. These responses take place every day, but happen so slowly we rarely notice them.

Dancing to the light

During the course of 24 hours some plants noticeably twirl, bend and move, all to position their leaves in the most light possible. These movements in response to the daily pattern of dark and light are known as phototropisms, and they can be revealed using time-lapse photography.

Light and animals

If you have ever been woken in the night by your pet hamster running furiously in its exercise wheel, you will know that plants are not the only living things affected by light. The waking and sleeping patterns of all sorts of animals, including birds, are affected by the changes in light levels over 24 hours. Many animals, ourselves included, are **diurnal** – they will naturally tend to wake up when it gets light and go to sleep as darkness falls.

Showing their colours
Flowering plants, like this osteospermum, rely on insects to pollinate their flowers, so they open up their coloured petals only during daylight, when the insects are about.

Other species react in exactly the opposite way – nocturnal animals sleep during the hours of daylight, and wake up and are active during the hours of darkness.

Nocturnal animals may have large eyes that are adapted to work with low light levels, or rely on other senses such as hearing, sonar (a specialized form of echolocation) or scent as their main way of finding out what is happening around them.

Changes in the length of the daylight hours also trigger seasonal changes in many living things. Trees lose their leaves and become dormant (stop growing) as the hours of light shorten and they can no longer make enough food by photosynthesis. Other garden and wild plants die back or disappear completely in winter.

The 24-hour body clock

Most living things, not only hamsters, show **circadian rhythms**. These are cycles of behaviour repeated approximately every 24 hours. The biological clocks that control the activities seem to be set by exposure to daylight. If organisms are kept in constant dark or constant light the rhythms tend to become either slightly shorter or slightly longer. So normal patterns of day and night are vital for most living organisms to function properly for any length of time.

Hibernation

In some countries the shorter days also trigger **hibernation** in animals like hedgehogs and squirrels – they feed frantically to build up fat before passing the winter in a deep sleep. As spring approaches, animals also have their own responses to the lengthening days. Your pet dog or cat sheds its thick winter coat and animals everywhere get down to the serious business of finding a mate and reproducing. Plants respond, too, as the buds swell and open in the garden and seeds germinate in the soil.

Did you know?

It is well known that some animals hibernate during winter to avoid the cold and lack of food. In some countries there are animals which 'switch off' through the summer months, usually by burrowing deep into mud, slowing down the body processes and waiting for cooler, wetter weather to return. This summer 'sleeping' is called 'aestivation'. For example, some frogs burrow deep into the mud and sleep away the hot dry months.

Light and communication

We enjoy the colours of flowers. Flowers are a plant's sex organs, displaying colours to attract insects. Looking closely, we can often see more subtle colours, patterns and markings on the petals, signposts for insects to direct them deep into the flower. Some flowers have markings we cannot see, however hard we look, because the patterns are in **ultraviolet**, and although we cannot see ultraviolet light, many of the insects that visit the flowers certainly can. This is just one example of the use of light as communication in living organisms.

Biological light

Depending where you live, you may see fireflies twinkling, lighting up trees with rapid flashes of brilliant light, or the steady glow of a glow-worm in the bottom of a hedge. It is astonishing that living things can create such light; and these insects are not on their own. Organisms ranging from seaweeds and mushrooms to insects and fish can produce this **bioluminescence** – wherever it occurs it is both fascinating and exciting.

Bioluminescence results from a chemical reaction in special light-producing cells. If the chemicals involved are extracted from the living cells and mixed together in the lab, the same light appears.

Fireflies in a tree
Bioluminescence is used to communicate messages such as 'I want a mate' or 'I taste horrible'.

Bioluminescence is used in many types of communication. Deep at sea, fish use it to see, to keep shoals together, to lure prey and to escape **predators**. Some toadstools and mushrooms use it to attract insects that will help them reproduce, while fireflies use it to repel predators when they are **larvae**, but to attract a mate when they are adult. This biological light really is one of Nature's wonders!

Navigating using the Sun

If you sit outside in a garden or park in summer you may hear the buzzing of bees in the flowers as they collect nectar to make honey. How do they know where to find it?

Scientists have learnt that bees have an amazing communication system that allows a bee that has found a patch of flowers to tell other bees in the hive where to find it. This system of the bees is based on the position of the Sun. Bees are amazingly sensitive to light from the Sun and the direction from which it comes.

Dancing bees

In the famous waggle dance, a worker bee that has found a good source of food can communicate that information to other bees. She registers the angle of the Sun to the flowers and informs the other bees during a dance on the combs of the hive. The other bees use that information as they leave the hive to navigate to the food.

Light dancing
This bee is 'dancing' to show the angle between the food source she has found and the Sun. She moves in a figure of eight and waggles her body to tell the other bees how far away the food is – the faster the waggle, the closer the food.

Did you know?

Bees are not the only animals that navigate using the Sun. Some birds visit us only in the winter or the summer, and fly thousands of miles to other continents for the remainder of the year. They have a sensitivity to the Earth's magnetic fields, and to the position of the Sun in the sky.

Light in the future

This book has shown how important light is in our everyday lives. But if we try to look into the future, it seems that light is going to be even more important in years to come. In 50 years' time it may seem laughable that light was such an under-used resource in the early 21st century!

Light mobiles

Do you have a mobile phone? If not, you almost certainly know someone who does. The use of mobile phones has absolutely rocketed in the last ten years – and new technology looks set to deliver faster and more secure networks in the years to come. The idea is that the cell phones of the future will use optical signals, linked through a fibre optic system. Scientists are already working on the technology needed to convert the radio signals from the handset directly into optical signals. We may talk to one another through an optical rather than an electronic system.

Mobile phones
The mobile phones of tomorrow may use visible light to carry our conversations and text messages.

The intelligent home

When you move about your home, you are probably fairly safe and unlikely to have an accident. However, the population of countries like the USA and the UK is getting steadily older – people are living longer and fewer babies are being born. Most older people want to maintain an independent lifestyle as long as they possibly can, but illness or problems such as failing sight can make it difficult for them to manage without support. However, research in the USA is moving rapidly to try to develop homes that can help to 'care' for older people, and can keep them independent for longer.

Many different developments make this possible, and many of them are modifications of existing systems, using infrared movement sensors and tiny cameras. If an elderly person wears a special piece of jewellery containing light-sensitive equipment, and has a number of monitors around their home, their movement can be monitored at a distance. Although they lose some privacy, they can remain safely in their own homes for longer, because alarms are triggered if they fall, or stay still in one place for too long, so then helpers will ring or visit to check that all is well. A family living at a distance could even have a 'portrait' of an elderly relative linked to the intelligent home system. Icons on the portrait would allow them to check up on grandma and see if she was busy, asleep, out and about or cooking. If they had any concerns, they could ring directly or contact a carer.

Blue movies?

The DVDs we use today are based on using red light to retrieve the stored data and they can hold around 4.7 gigabytes of information in the pits made on the surface. New technology being developed uses blue light to read the information on the DVD. Blue light has a much shorter wavelength than red light, so much smaller pits can be burnt into the disc. This means more information can be coded onto the same area. So using blue light, it is hoped that in future it will be possible to store about five times as much information on a disc.

The quantum computer

New technologies using light are set to change all our lives over the next twenty years, let alone the next century. Undoubtedly, the biggest changes will come as a result of the development of **quantum computers**, if that proves possible.

Computing using light

What is meant by a quantum computer? Think about the computer you use for playing games on or for doing school work. These conventional computers use fundamental bits of information – 1 and 0 – as the basis of their digital function. These bits of information are physically recorded within the machine, and so there are physical limits to the amount of information we can store and the speed with which we can retrieve it.

Scientists are trying to develop a new generation of computers that they hope will overcome the problems of the ones we use today. Quantum computers will use the power of light and the properties of atoms themselves to perform memory and processing tasks. If their predictions are correct, the computers of tomorrow could be billions of times faster and more powerful than the computers of today.

Richard Feynman 1918-88

US scientist Richard P. Feynman was one of the first people to recognize the potential in quantum physics for solving problems much, much faster than had ever been thought possible – in other words, to imagine a quantum computer! Feynman was one of the great scientists of our time. He specialized in the study of the structure of matter. His ideas ranged from nuclear physics to quantum computers and he won a Nobel prize for his work on the way particles interact. Feynman was a larger-than-life personality as well. When he died in 1988 his students at the California Institute of Technology hung a banner from the library proclaiming simply 'We love you, Dick' – a tribute to his humanity as much as his scientific brilliance!

Computer dinosaur
In twenty years' time modern computers will look as ridiculous as this enormous one, built in the 1940s, does to us now, as tiny, light-controlled computers take over.

How will a quantum computer work?

Quantum computers will work in a remarkably similar way to conventional computers, except that the information will be coded using **photons** of light (**quantum** particles or **qubits**). Using quantum physics, these machines will be able to work on millions of computations at once – they will be vastly more powerful than any computers even dreamed of today.

Because a quantum computer is based on such unbelievably tiny particles, it has the potential to be millions of times more powerful than today's most powerful supercomputers. Unfortunately, the technology needed to develop these computers that work in the quantum world of light does not yet exist – the basic steps that have been taken so far are the computer equivalent of 1 + 1! But scientists predict that by 2050 quantum computers will be running our lives!

The light fantastic

Light is a fundamental part of our everyday lives. It allows us to see, it gives everything colour and form, and it provides us with food, both directly and indirectly. We create light artificially and use light in countless gadgets and tools. Finding out about the nature of light has inspired some of the greatest scientists of all time, and light drives our research into technology that will make life better in future. An understanding of light not only gives us a better understanding of the world around us, but also opens our eyes to possibilities beyond our wildest dreams.

Summary: everything is illuminated

Playing with fire
Fireworks, with their bright light and glorious colours, have been used in celebrations for centuries, since the Chinese first invented them.

Light is an integral part of life on Earth. Most of us are aware of light because we can see. Our eyes are complex organs that respond to light and give us a visual picture of the world. To explore anywhere – from the depths of a cave to the inside of the human body – we need light.

Special instruments make it possible to take a small light deep into the human body, to allow doctors to see any problems that may be developing. They can see what is going on because a tiny camera is also passed into the body and the images are relayed to the doctor, often using **optical fibres** because they are so fine.

The nature of light is complex – and **visible light** forms only part of the **electromagnetic spectrum**. Scientists have worked for centuries to give us our current understanding of the properties of light. From the early explanations of the rainbow to the **quantum** physics of today, our increasing knowledge of the nature of light has lead to the development of more and more light-based technology.

Light reaches our Earth from space, from the Sun, the Moon and the stars. Some of the light we see has travelled billions of miles over millions of years. This light enables us to see, and the changes in the length of the daylight through the seasons of the year control the cycles of nature. The world around us is full of colour, and those colours are dependant on the way different wavelengths of light are reflected or absorbed. Wherever we look, in our everyday lives and in the furthest corners of the Universe, light is there, playing a vital role. As technology develops over the next fifty years, it is likely to become more important still.

Glossary

bioluminescence light produced by living organisms

blind spot place on the retina without light-sensitive cells, where the optic nerve leaves the eye

cataract lens of the eye when it has gone cloudy owing to the accumulation of dead and damaged tissue

chlorophyll green pigment in plants that captures light energy for photosynthesis

circadian rhythms cycles in the behaviour and physiology of organisms that last about 24 hours

cones light-sensitive cells in the retina of the eye that respond to high-intensity, coloured light

diffraction waves spreading out when they pass through a narrow slit

dilate widen or expand (a body part)

dispersion separation of white light into colours

diurnal active during the day

electromagnetic spectrum complete range of electromagnetic radiation: gamma rays, X-rays, ultraviolet radiation, visible light, infrared radiation, microwaves and radio waves

electrons subatomic particles with a negative charge

energy capacity to do work

hibernate sleep deeply or remain inactive during winter, to survive difficult conditions

iris coloured part of the eye that controls the size of the pupil

larvae (plural of larva) immature form of an insect

laser device that produces an intense beam of light. Taken from the initials of: Light Amplification by the Stimulated Emission of Radiation

light year distance travelled by a ray of light in one year in a vacuum

lunar eclipse event occurring when the Moon moves into the shadow of the Earth

opaque not letting light through

optic nerve nerve that carries nerve messages from the retina of the eye to the brain

optical fibres thin flexible transport fibres, usually made of glass or plastic, through which light can be transmitted. They are used extensively in telecommunications.

optical illusion image that fools the brain into 'seeing' something that is not there

penumbra shadow between the area of complete illumination and the area of complete shadow

photochemical decomposition breakdown of chemical substance when exposed to light

photon packet of electromagnetic radiation energy, such as light

photosynthesis process by which plants make food from carbon dioxide and water, using energy from the Sun captured using chlorophyll

pinhole camera simple camera that lets in light through a small hole

predator animal that preys on other animals

prism solid block of transparent material, such as glass, in which the ends are matching parallel polygrams and all other surfaces are parallelograms

pupil dark hole in the middle of the iris that lets light into the eye

quantum smallest quantity of energy

quantum computer cutting-edge computer technology in the very earliest stages of development, involving subatomic particles

quantum theory theory that describes the nature of matter and energy

qubit quantum bit. It is the quantum computer equivalent of the binary digit or bit in normal computing.

reflect bounce (a wave) sound, light or heat back from a surface

refract bend a beam of light as it passes from one material to another of different density, e.g. from air to water

retina layer of light-sensitive cells at the back of the eye that reacts both to the presence and to the colour of light

rods light-sensitive cells in the retina of the eye that are sensitive to low-intensity light

shadow dark area formed behind an object that is blocking light rays

solar eclipse event occurring when the Moon passes between the Earth and the Sun, blocking out the Sun from an area of the Earth's surface

spectrum arrangement of electromagnetic waves by wavelengths and frequencies

translucent (of a material) allowing some, but not all, light to pass through it, so that we cannot see through it

transparent (of a material) allowing almost all light to pass through it, so that it is 'see-through'

ultraviolet electromagnetic radiation with a wavelength just beyond the violet (short-wave) end of the visible spectrum

umbra dark central area of a shadow where no light falls at all

vacuum space containing nothing

visible light (also called white light) the part of the electromagnetic spectrum visible to human eyes

wave-particle duality observed behaviour of light (and other electromagnetic radiation) either as a wave (when that model best describes the behaviour) or as a particle (when that is a better model)

white light (also called visible light) the part of the electromagnetic spectrum visible to human eyes

Finding out more

Books

The Dorling Kindersley Science Encyclopedia, (Dorling Kindersley, 1999)

Fascinating Science Projects: Light, by Sally Hewitt (Franklin Watts, 2002)

Groundbreakers: Isaac Newton, by Tony Allen (Heinemann Library, 2001)

Science Files: Light, by Steve Parker (Heinemann Library, 2004)

Science, The Facts: Light, by Rebecca Hunter (Franklin Watts, 2003)

Science Topics: Light and Sound, by Chris Oxlade and Ann Fullick (Heinemann Library, 1999)

20th Century Media: Sound and Light, by Steve Parker (Heinemann Library, 2003)

Websites

www.sciencemuseum.org.uk
This gives access to the Science Museum website, where lots of information about light can be found.

www.lightwave.soton.ac.uk
This wacky, fun website is from the people at Southampton University, UK. It includes all sorts of information on light.

www.why-is-the-sky-blue.org
This is a really interesting site which sets out to answer lots of questions about light and other aspects of science.

www.encarta.msn.com/encnet/refpages/artcenter.aspx
Encarta is a great resource with lots of information about light, colour, vision and all the other topics in this book.

Index